Modern Foreign Languages

A review of inspection findings 1993/94

A report from the Office of Her Majesty's Chief Inspector of Schools

London: HMSO

ISBN 0 11 350056 4

Office for Standards in Education
Alexandra House
29–33 Kingsway
London WC2B 6SE

Telephone 0171-421 6800

Contents

Annex B

GCE AS and A-level results for Modern Foreign Languages 1994

Introduction

This subject profile provides a review of the findings from inspection conducted for and by OFSTED during the academic year 1993/94. It continues the publication by OFSTED of subject reports focused on the quality of provision made for, and standards of achievement in, modern foreign languages.[1] It extends information and discussion to include aspects of inspecting modern foreign languages which are of direct interest to inspectors and may also be found relevant by schools.

The evaluation of standards, quality of education and provision for modern foreign languages is based on evidence from inspection of maintained secondary schools undertaken in that period.

The modern foreign language profile is based mainly on evidence drawn from OFSTED inspection of 735 secondary schools conducted by independent inspectors. Reference has also been made to Her Majesty's Inspectors of Schools (HMI) evidence drawn from the inspection visits of 60 schools in the period September 1993 to June 1994. The statistical statements about lesson grades are based only on the OFSTED inspections conducted by independent inspectors. The illustrative statements on lessons and the comments on contributory factors are drawn mainly from OFSTED inspections conducted by independent inspectors. Evidence from the inspection of modern foreign languages in secondary schools by specialist HMI was used to assist in the interpretation of patterns emerging from the main body of inspection data.

Modern foreign languages is not a compulsory subject in the National Curriculum before Key Stage 3. In 1993/94 National Curriculum requirements applied only to Years 7 and 8.

---

[1] Modern Foreign Languages, Key Stage 3, First Year 1992–93, HMSO, 1993.

Subject Report

Main Findings

- Standards of achievement are generally lower in Key Stage 4 than in Key Stage 3 or in the sixth form (paragraphs 1, 4 and 7).

- Within Key Stage 3 standards of achievement are better in Years 7 and 8 than in Year 9 (paragraph 1).

- The target language is used more by teachers in Key Stage 3 than in Key Stage 4, but its use by pupils is underdeveloped in both Key Stages (paragraphs 2, 3, 5 and 6).

- The range of teaching styles is beginning to be influenced by the Programmes of Study (paragraph 10).

- The quality of curricular planning is better in Years 7 and 8 than in later years (paragraph 24).

- In most schools the National Curriculum is influencing the way in which pupils' attainments are assessed and recorded in Years 7 and 8 but assessment is not often used formatively (paragraphs 15 and 16).

- Over half of the schools require all pupils to study a modern foreign language in Key Stage 4 (paragraph 20).

- Sixth form students are generally competent linguistically but the range of attainment is wide and some experience considerable difficulty in the transition from Key Stage 4 (paragraph 8).

- The teachers' command of the subject is good and the deployment of their skills effective in the vast majority of schools, but more attention needs to be paid to staff development in the weaker departments (paragraphs 28 and 29).

Key issues for schools

- The improvement of standards, particularly in Key Stage 4.

- The further adjustment of teaching styles to deliver the range of opportunities set out in the Programmes of Study.

- The development of the use of the target language by pupils, and the continued improvement in its use by teachers.

- The further development of assessment policies and practices appropriate for the delivery of the National Curriculum.

- The improvement of continuity and progression between Key Stage 4 and the sixth form.

- Staff development to improve teachers' specialist skills and the effectiveness of their deployment in the weaker departments.

Standards of achievement

The GCSE and GCE results achieved nationally in Modern Foreign Languages in 1994 are addressed in a section commencing at paragraph 56.

Key Stage 3

1   Standards achieved in relation to pupils' capabilities were satisfactory or better in 78% of lessons and good in 30%, compared with 81% and 31% respectively for lessons in all subjects. Standards were lower in modern foreign languages in Year 9 than in Years 7 or 8 and pupils' response was markedly better in upper ability than in mixed, middle and lower ability groups.

2   Pupils' progress was usually more marked in listening and speaking than in reading or writing. The most developed skill was the ability to understand the spoken language. Pupils were able to follow without difficulty lessons competently conducted in the target language, although the level of challenge was not always significantly raised during the Key Stage. Standards of pronunciation were usually sound. Most pupils could use the vocabulary and phrases they had learned for basic communication, but their ability to apply their knowledge in new

situations was limited. Within the limited range of texts that they were expected to read, almost exclusively short extracts from textbooks or worksheets, they could usually extract basic information. Written work was usually well presented. Pupils showed reasonable accuracy in combining familiar words and phrases, but much less when they had to compose new sentences to express their own ideas; many pupils did not pay sufficient attention to accuracy in their writing. Occasionally, pupils were expected to undertake more extended or creative written tasks and more able pupils in particular rose well to this challenge.

3   Most pupils showed a positive attitude to learning a foreign language, particularly where they were constantly and actively involved. They usually co-operated well and persevered with concentration in individual tasks. However, unwillingness to listen attentively in a minority of cases and, rather more frequently, to refrain from distracting chatter in English during pair or group work, was especially damaging to effective learning. While pupils were willing to speak the foreign language when expressly required, very few did so spontaneously; it was rare for them to take the initiative in speaking or to attempt longer utterances.

Key Stage 4

4   Standards achieved in relation to pupils' capabilities were satisfactory or better in 74% of lessons and good in 26%, compared with 83% and 32% respectively for lessons in all subjects. A third of lessons with less able pupils were less than satisfactory.

5   Standards at Key Stage 4 showed insufficient progression from Key Stage 3 and many of the features characterising performance at the earlier stage continued to be present. Increased knowledge was more evident in a larger vocabulary than in a wider range of expression based on a sure grasp of grammar. Where pupils had this security, they were able to communicate effectively and had the confidence to speak at greater length, whereas others continued to respond as briefly as possible. Pupils could understand the spoken language but, partly because teachers spoke less frequently in the target language than in Key Stage 3, the demands on their listening were often too low. As the range of written texts was similar to that offered in Key Stage 3, pupils were rarely expected to demonstrate a capacity for extended reading or to

extract information from more complex texts. Written work, though usually well presented, varied in accuracy and consisted mainly of short paragraphs or dialogue. Where opportunities were provided, pupils showed that they could undertake longer and more demanding tasks with success. In many aspects of their work, pupils could have achieved higher standards if they had encountered and retained a wider range of vocabulary and structure in the earlier years.

6 Pupils' attitudes were usually positive, but the enthusiasm evident in many beginners' lessons was less often apparent at Key Stage 4. Often pupils were not making significant progress in using language skills. They were often more reticent in speaking than younger pupils. They showed less inclination to use the target language as a direct medium of communication with the teacher or each other. They made more use of authentic material, but older learners were no more likely to engage in extended reading for content: most use of written text was for formal comprehension purposes. Writing increased in length, but was still confined largely to the same basic, personal topics as before (such as introductory letters to penfriends).

Post-16

7 Standards achieved in relation to students' capabilities were satisfactory or better in 89% of lessons and good in 40%, compared with 91% and 42% for lessons in all subjects.

8 The standard of listening comprehension was usually sound and often good. Students generally showed interest and commitment. In the best cases, and where expectations were high, students displayed fluency in speaking and an ability to participate fully in discussion, arguing their point of view. This contrasted with other cases in which students showed a lack of confidence in speaking: they appeared to understand the foreign language reasonably well, but lacked the confidence to attempt more than short statements. These difficulties may have originated in an inadequate preparation at Key Stage 4. Students could usually understand literary and non-literary texts without difficulty and could write, though with variable accuracy, on a range of topics. Whilst the best writing was impressive, some students struggled to cope with the increased demands of sixth form work.

Quality of teaching

Key Stage 3

9   The quality of teaching was satisfactory or better in 77% of lessons and good in 39%, compared with 81% and 42% respectively for lessons in all subjects.

10   Most lessons had relevant objectives for which varied learning activities had been planned in some detail, but these objectives were not always sufficiently clear to pupils. Key Stage 3 lesson planning broadly followed the Programmes of Study, though with varying emphasis on the four Attainment Targets: reading, in particular the development of independent reading of books, was generally neglected; writing was often limited in range. In the more effective lessons, varied resources, including some authentic materials, were used. Teachers' competence in the target language was sound in the great majority of cases and most were striving to use it extensively in their teaching as required by the Programmes of Study, though only rarely was such practice fully consistent across a department. However, teachers either gave insufficient opportunity for, or did not insist firmly enough on, pupils using the target language themselves. Most teachers used a range of styles, including whole class, pair and group work, though very often there was insufficient opportunity for pupils to master new language adequately, through intensive practice, before being required to use it in more independent work. This sometimes reduced the effectiveness of pair and group work. Lack of differentiation led to inappropriate expectations of abler pupils in particular.

Key Stage 4

11   The quality of teaching was satisfactory or better in 78% of lessons and good in 37%, compared with 83% and 43% respectively for lessons in all subjects.

12   There was less consistent use of the target language by teachers in Key Stage 4 than in Key Stage 3 and rarer challenging of pupils to use it. In some schools where teachers had appropriate expectations of their Key Stage 3 pupils, they did not make correspondingly higher demands on older pupils. Often they did not provide pupils with the

opportunity for more creative and extended speaking. Few modern languages departments had wholly consistent practice in the essential elements of methodology: thus parallel groups of pupils within the same school often had very contrasting learning experiences.

Post-16

13   In sixth forms, teaching was satisfactory or better in 88% of lessons and good in 51%, compared with 89% and 52% respectively for lessons in all subjects.

14   Lessons were usually well planned and the majority were taught largely in the target language. In the best lessons, teachers used a variety of methods and resources and encouraged the students to work in groups and to take the initiative in discussion.

Assessment, recording and reporting

15   The National Curriculum was influencing the ways in which pupils' attainments were assessed and recorded in Years 7 and 8 in almost all schools. Some relied heavily on assessment materials provided by the commercial course used, but in others considerable attention was being paid to devising tasks and tests and to determining the potential of planned, routine activities to furnish evidence of pupils' levels of attainment.

16   Some progress was being made by teachers in applying the criteria of National Curriculum assessment continuously in their routine observation of pupils' performance in class. Sometimes this was linked to discussion within and between schools aimed at establishing a common understanding of Statements of Attainment and agreement about the nature of evidence. Assessment was occasionally being put to formative use. In all these areas, however, there was still much more to do. Few schools were developing portfolios of exemplar material for assessment purposes.

17   Most schools were developing satisfactory systems of recording the progress of pupils in Years 7 and 8, in some cases after abandoning procedures which had proved unmanageable. Beyond Year 8, recording was less comprehensive than in those years to which National Curriculum requirements already applied.

18   The marking of pupils' written work was usually regular and positive. There were instances of very helpful comment, both oral and written, but more often pupils had inadequate guidance on how to improve.

19   A common weakness in reporting to parents was the tendency to comment on a pupil's attitude and effort at the expense of precise statements about attainment.

Curriculum content

20   The requirements of the National Curriculum for modern foreign languages were complied with in Key Stage 3: all pupils studied one or more modern foreign languages. Over half of the schools required all pupils to study a modern foreign language in Key Stage 4. Overall time allocations for modern foreign languages were generally satisfactory in both Key Stages; exceptions included some schools which divided the available time between two modern foreign languages in Key Stage 3 so that insufficient time was spent on each.

21   Although most schools introduced some or all of their pupils to a second modern foreign language during Key Stage 3, a small minority did not offer this possibility in either Key Stage. In most schools the numbers studying more than one modern foreign language in Key Stage 4 were low.

22   Many schools had diversified their provision to introduce German or Spanish as a first modern foreign language alongside French. A few, however, had been obliged to modify or abandon such arrangements, at least temporarily, because of staffing difficulties.

23   Setting by attainment in modern foreign languages was usual from Year 8 onwards. This was helpful to learning but not sufficient in itself to ensure adequate differentiation. Whether groups were setted or not, differentiation was often neglected in lesson planning.

24   The majority of schemes of work showed clearly the influence of the National Curriculum and provided sound guidance to teachers. Course planning for Years 7 and 8 was usually better than that for later years and it often made detailed reference to the Programmes of Study and Attainment Targets. However, some areas received insufficient

attention, for example, opportunities for reading and topics or activities which engaged pupils' imagination or creativity. A great deal of learning in Key Stage 3 was limited to Areas of Experience A and B of the Programmes of Study Part II. Schemes of work needed to pay more attention to ensuring progression, particularly at Key Stage 4. Where schemes of work gave sound guidance, this was not always implemented by teachers: for example, the use of the target language by teachers and pupils was inconsistent and the range of resources used was narrow.

Provision for pupils with special educational needs

25   The allocation of extra staff time to support pupils with special educational needs in modern foreign language classes varied greatly in quantity and in effectiveness. It was more effective where the support staff had modern foreign language expertise, where help was targeted on particular pupils, and where there was substantial liaison in planning and the preparation of materials. In planning, setting was often presumed to cater sufficiently, or to make a substantial contribution to providing, for pupils with special educational needs; this was usually not the case in practice.

26   Although some schools provided 'extension' materials for abler pupils, very few planned or catered for the special needs of the most able.

Management and administration

27   The quality of management and co-ordination of modern foreign language teaching was good in the great majority of schools. Successful departments were characterised by firm leadership and a shared sense of purpose underpinned by clear documentation and procedures. In the weaker departments, routine administration was usually more effective than development planning and policies tended to be ill defined or inconsistently implemented. The discipline of implementing the National Curriculum had beneficial effects on planning, but insufficient attention was paid to Part I of the Programmes of Study. In some

of the weaker departments, there was little or no self-evaluation and it was underdeveloped elsewhere.

Resources and their management

Teaching staff

28   The teachers' command of the subject was good and the deployment of their specialist skills effective in the vast majority of schools. Where deployment was not effective, classes tended to be taught by non-specialist teachers or specialists teaching their weaker foreign language. Teachers whose command of the subject was weak were usually insecure in the use of the target language.

29   In the weaker departments more attention needed to be paid to staff development, providing access to a wider range of INSET (including linguistic refreshment), and meeting the needs of part-time and non-specialist staff.

30   Only a minority of modern foreign language departments had access to non-teaching support. Ancillary support in the modern foreign language classroom was usually deployed with pupils with special educational needs and was less likely to be available in Key Stage 4 than in Key Stage 3. The contribution of non-teaching staff was effective in the majority of schools where they were available to support work in modern foreign languages.

Resources for learning

31   The quality of learning resources was good and their use effective in the majority of schools. The level of resources varied considerably between departments and the weaker departments were less likely to have an appropriate range of resources available and accessible. However, there was no consistent association between the overall level of resources on the one hand and the quality of the teaching and learning and the standards achieved on the other.

32   The main resources used were the coursebook, tape recordings and flashcards linked to it, and worksheets leading to oral or written work. The overhead projector was sometimes used as an aid to comprehension to support the development of the use of the target language,

but more limited use was made of video. The use of information technology in modern foreign language classes was frequently underdeveloped. This was sometimes due to shortages of equipment, but more often to other factors including limited access to facilities, lack of IT expertise among the teachers, or inadequate planning to deliver the Programmes of Study.

33   It was rare for pupils to have opportunities to develop independence in their use of equipment and materials as required by the Programmes of Study. This was more difficult in schools where pupils did not each have a textbook in their keeping or where there was insufficient access to suitable reference materials.

Accommodation

34   The availability of accommodation was good and its use effective in the majority of schools.

35   There was no consistent association between the accommodation used and the quality of teaching and learning and standards achieved. However, the weaker departments were more likely to suffer from cramped or dispersed rooms which inhibited the range of activities or access to equipment. The quality of the acoustics frequently presented difficulties and even in the better departments this affected work in some classrooms. Other factors included inadequate blackout for the use of visual aids and poorly located power supplies which inhibited the use of equipment. The use made of available accommodation varied considerably, for example in the range and quality of display.

Inspection issues

Inspection development

36   Inspections carried out under Section 9 of the Education (Schools) Act 1992 began in September 1993. Inspection teams have made a good start in meeting the demanding requirements of the Framework for the Inspection of Schools; they have become more confident as the year has progressed and early uncertainties have been resolved in many cases. This part of the subject profile draws together some of the key issues for further improving the quality and standard of inspection. Many issues are similar from one subject to another but where there are subject-specific matters these are indicated.

37   Some examples of inspection writing are included. They are not intended to be viewed as models or templates but have been chosen to illustrate how the Framework and inspection documentation requirements can be reasonably met.

Evidence gathering

38   Inspectors usually sample a good range of work in modern foreign languages of different year groups, abilities and Key Stages across the compulsory years of education. They usually achieve a good balance although the time allocated to inspecting languages varies considerably. It is important that where a school has a sixth form, post-16 work is fairly represented in the sampling.

39   In reaching their judgements, inspectors use evidence from a good range of sources. It is particularly important in modern foreign languages that evidence of written work encountered outside the lessons observed should receive due emphasis and that clear reference is made to it to support judgements in records of evidence. The Supplementary Evidence Form provides a means of documenting evidence and judgements from sources other than lessons and could be more widely used.

Lesson Observation Forms

40   Lesson Observation Forms are usually completed conscientiously, with attention to the relevant evaluation criteria. Inspectors could usefully check that subject detail and characteristics are incorporated into the judgements wherever possible.

41   The majority of inspectors indicate the content of lessons adequately, usually with reference to the National Curriculum Order, but sufficient detail of activities needs to be given to set the context for evaluation.

An example of a 'Content' section from a Lesson Observation Form follows.

> *Year 8 German Upper ability*
>
> *House and home – describing house, rooms, etc. PoS AoE A and C; range of PoS I. AT1.1-3, AT 2.1-3, AT4.1-2*
>
> *Oral practice and application – with team games/activities, focusing on case endings and word order. Leads to written consolidation exercise, then further language practice activities. NB The pupils are in their first term of German.*

42   Inspectors draw on their professional knowledge and experience to make overall judgements about the **achievements** of pupils. Responding to the Framework requirements to assess pupils' achievements in relation to national expectations and taking account of pupils' abilities has not proved easy. Revised requirements and guidance published in June 1994 should help inspectors in making these distinct judgements. To support judgements it is important that inspectors clearly identify and record what pupils know, understand and can do and set achievements in the context of National Curriculum Statements of Attainment.

43   In modern foreign language lessons, it is particularly important that there is evidence of how well pupils can understand and respond to, and communicate in, the target language, and that this evidence is related to the Attainment Target Levels achieved. Brief examples of the language used by pupils are a useful means of demonstrating the basis of the judgement at the level of achievement.

44   An extract from an 'Achievement' section from a Lesson Observation Form follows.

Year 10 Spanish Middle ability

Achievement (age referenced): Pupils display standards which are at least satisfactory in terms of national expectations. They speak readily with a good accent and intonation, can initiate language and understand quite a wide range of instructions. They write simple but accurate Spanish.
Grade: 3

Achievement (relating to pupils' abilities): The pupils are all, with one exception, reaching a good standard or better in terms of their capabilities. Retention is good, and language production accurate and confident.
Grade: 2

45   Clear evidence of pupils' attitudes to learning and their behaviour in lessons is usually given, and this is reflected in the grade given for **quality of learning.** Greater prominence should be given to other important attributes of learning, particularly pupils' progress in lessons and the aspects of learning included in sections 3.2 and 6.8 of Part 4 of the *Handbook for the Inspection of Schools*. An example of a 'Learning' section from a Lesson Observation Form follows.

Year 8 German Upper ability

Very intense involvement. They work very well in pairs. They are making clear progress in putting more complex questions. They are in no way intimidated by the authentic text but simply complete the task. Able to use dictionaries. Again not intimidated by high level listening task. They simply listen hard. Grade: 1

46   The criteria for the quality of teaching in the Framework are usually used appropriately and relevant evidence is cited. The teachers' readiness to use the target language and their expectations of its use by pupils are important elements in the evaluation of teaching. The impact of teaching on pupils' achievements and the quality of learning sometimes need to be made more explicit. An example of a 'Teaching' section from a Lesson Observation Form follows.

Year 9 French Middle ability

Objectives fairly low level. Teacher does not convey high expectations. Over-dependence on use of English. No established pattern of use of target language. Teaching does not create and sustain interest and motivation, lacks pace and sense of direction. Does not challenge pupils' thinking or promote extension of skills. Quite good on one-to-one support and encouragement (with lots of English). Teacher's MFL competence sound. Grade: 4

47   Lesson Observation Forms also provide opportunity to signal the impact of contributory factors on achievements and the quality of learning which can be drawn on when compiling the Subject Evidence Form.

Subject Evidence Forms

48   Subject Evidence Forms are usually fully completed. In most cases, a wide range of evidence appears to have been used. Inspectors need to check that reference to the range of evidence underpinning the judgements is sufficiently explicit in the relevant sections of the form and to ensure that the emphasis is on evaluation rather than description.

49   Particular attention is given to aspects of standards of achievement and the quality of learning and teaching although, as in Lesson Observation Forms, in considering the quality of learning more emphasis is placed on pupils' attitudes and behaviour than on their skills as learners. When commenting on examination results as part of their evaluation of standards of achievement, inspectors should ensure that the evidence includes the basis for any comparisons with national data. When dealing with standards more generally, it is important to exemplify the language skills shown by pupils and, where schools have sixth forms, to comment explicitly about post-16 standards and quality.

50   An extract from a 'Standards of achievement' section from a Subject Evidence Form follows.

Key Stage 3

There was a marked variation in standards of achievement from lesson to lesson. In the majority of lessons observed (64%), standards relative to national expectation and pupils' abilities were satisfactory or better; in no lessons observed were they very good.

In most classes, pupils were able to use and understand a limited range of the target language (gist, specific details, identify main points) in familiar settings. A number of pupils were able to initiate and sustain a conversation. Pronunciation was generally intelligible and sometimes good. The level of grammatical accuracy was rarely better than satisfactory. There was little spontaneous, independent use of the language.

In some lessons, however, there was a marked under-performance in all skills. Pupils' grasp and retention of vocabulary and structure (particularly that covered in recent weeks) was weak. In such cases, understanding was very limited and pupils were unable to respond effectively except to very low-level questions, usually with short fixed utterances. They were unable to adapt memorised language; they lacked confidence; they retained insufficient language and had insufficient skills to communicate effectively.

Key Stage 4

In the majority of lessons observed (78%), standards relative to national expectations and pupils' abilities were satisfactory or good; in no lesson observed were they very good and there were few outstanding performances by individual pupils. In some lessons, pupils showed competence in understanding and responding to spoken and written language. Several pupils were able to use more complex language; to handle more extended utterances, including less familiar language and an element of the unpredictable; to adapt language to new situations. A number of pupils were able to take some initiative and to ask for help and seek clarification - although not as many as might have been expected. They showed a grasp of underlying pattern and structure. In general, production (speaking and writing) was less secure than listening, and written skills and written accuracy were underdeveloped. In a minority of lessons, especially those involving less able pupils, pupils' command of grammar and vocabulary was weak; there was little evidence of progression beyond the basics; understanding was poor; pupils were unable to respond to simple questions or to sustain a conversation.

Post-16

In the A-level lessons observed, standards were good. Pupils were able to understand a wide range of complex and demanding language. They communicated effectively and showed a good range of vocabulary and structure and a growing awareness of styles and registers. They were lexically accurate, although spelling and grammatical accuracy were less good in Year 12. Several pupils could converse fluently and accurately, developing an argument, expressing and defending opinions, persuading, drawing inferences.

51   When considering contributory factors such as the resources for learning, management and the quality of teaching, the emphasis should be on evaluation of the impact they have on the standards achieved by pupils and the quality of learning. The following extract from a 'Contributory factors' section of the Subject Evidence Form includes judgements on features of provision and some indications of effects.

Assessment, Recording and Reporting

In Key Stage 3, work is assessed in accordance with statutory requirements. There is an excellent system of assessment and recording which is rooted in the Statements of Attainment. It defines what a pupil must know, understand and be able to do in relation to each Attainment Target, in each unit of work. Assessments are systematically recorded by pupils, as part of a formative process, which is manageable and understood by staff and pupils alike. Criteria for assessment are shared with pupils and displayed on the walls in all classrooms alongside pupil-friendly National Curriculum statements for each Attainment Target. Pupils have a general understanding of National Curriculum progress. Pupils are encouraged to self-assess, and with guidelines, translate raw marks into marks out of five and subsequently relate to National Curriculum attainment.

Judgement Recording Statements

52   The Judgement Recording Statements are usually fully completed. It is important that this is so and that all available evidence is considered in arriving at judgements. The purpose and use of Judgement Recording Statements need to be fully understood by all inspectors; these are outlined in Appendix C of Part 3 of the *Handbook for the Inspection of Schools*.

53   If a particular Judgement Recording Statement item does not apply, for example statutory requirements for assessment and recording in modern foreign languages in Key Stage 4 and post-16, it should be left blank.

Subject sections in inspection reports

54   Most subject sections in inspection reports meet the Framework requirements and are consistent with the evidence contained in the Subject Evidence Form. They give appropriate emphasis to comments on standards of achievement and the quality of learning and teaching, although more comment specific to modern foreign languages could sometimes be given to these sections. For example, some of these sections could have been strengthened by a clearer focus on the use of the target language by pupils. It is important that overall judgements are clear and succinct and draw on all the evidence available and that factors which have an impact on standards of achievement and quality of learning are clearly identified.

55   An example of an extract from a report follows.

Standards achieved at Key Stage 3 are similar to national expectations for most pupils, although there is under-achievement in some middle or lower ability groups. Mostly, pupils are confident in using a limited range of language. They have a sound grasp of vocabulary and structure. Pronunciation is satisfactory to good. They can understand the main points and identify relevant details in what they hear and read. Writing is under-developed. Where standards are less satisfactory, pupils lack confidence and fluency orally, are not able to use language skills in combination, and have a poor grasp of work recently covered.

At Key Stage 4, standards are similar to national expectations in most lessons. For some pupils they are good or very good, particularly in German; in lower ability groups, however, standards need to be raised. In general, listening skills are good. Many pupils are able to express what they want and choose to say within a reasonable range of topics, without being over-dependent on their teacher. This is a strength. Pupils are less able to express their own ideas in writing and the range of written tasks is too narrow.

In the sixth form, standards in A-level lessons are satisfactory. Most students can use the language to communicate effectively in spite of some inaccuracy.

The work seen in Key Stage 3 was in line with the requirements of the National Curriculum. There is a useful and detailed scheme of work for German which shows clearly how teachers plan to cover all aspects of the National Curriculum Programmes of Study. No such scheme exists for French, to provide evidence that over the year the Programme of Study will be adequately covered and to ensure that teachers are in a position to monitor this. This should be dealt with as a matter of urgency.

Pupils' attitudes are generally good. In the best lessons seen, pupils were setting high standards for themselves and looking critically at how they were performing in order to find ways of improving. In such lessons, the rate of work and progress were high. In some lessons, however, pupils were not sufficiently challenged by the work set and time was spent on activities which were not geared appropriately to increasing their knowledge of the language or improving their skills in speaking, listening, reading and writing. At times the work did not take enough account of what pupils already knew.

The quality of teaching was variable. In the majority of lessons, it was satisfactory or better. In some cases it was good or very good indeed. At best, it was lively and enthusiastic, conveying high expectations, with consistent use of the target language by the teacher and pupils. Whilst there was some systematic teaching of the words and phrases which pupils need in order to sustain the use of the target language in the classroom, not enough attention was paid to this. Where teaching was less than satisfactory, the pace was slow and the objectives were not sufficiently clear or relevant to the pupils. Usually in these cases, pupils had little contact with the target language and too few opportunities to use it for themselves.

Overall, the range of resources and equipment is adequate. However, there is a need for more up-to-date books and materials which take account of the requirements of the National Curriculum.

The management and co-ordination of the department need to be strengthened to improve the consistency of good practice.

The interpretation of subject performance data

56   The tables below show the key statistics on GCSE and A-level/AS results in modern foreign languages (French, German and Spanish). The individual schools results should be compared with those of schools of the same type and not with those recorded for 'all entries'.

57   In modern foreign languages particular care is needed concerning the following:

- variations between schools in take-up in Key Stage 4 and conse-quently in the size of the cohort entered for GCSE (it is often useful to compare both average points per entry and the average points per pupil at the school with the corresponding national statistics);

- variations in the performance of boys and girls (in general girls do better at GCSE, and boys do very slightly better at A-level);

- distinguishing between performance in the first modern foreign language and that in the second modern foreign language, for example in German, national statistics are skewed by the large proportion of mainly more able candidates taking German as a second modern foreign language and do not therefore provide a secure basis of comparison with results in a school where German is the first (or joint first) modern foreign language in Key Stage 4;

- the small numbers taking modern foreign languages at A-level in some schools which can make generalisation unreliable.

Annex A

GCSE results for 15 year olds[1] for French 1994

Type of School		Number of 15[1] year old pupils entered	1994													1993		1992[2]	
			Percentages achieving grades									Average points score[3]	% A*-C grades	% A*-G grades		Average points score[3]	% A-C grades	Average points score[3]	% A-C grades
			A*	A	B	C	D	E	F	G	U								
Comprehensive		237131	1.9	9.4	11.5	16.4	20.2	16.5	14.2	6.3	0.9	4.12	39.2	96.5		3.81	37.7	3.82	36.7
Selective		13222	11.5	37.5	24.0	15.6	7.8	2.4	0.8	0.1	0.0	6.18	88.6	99.7		6.04	89.3	5.92	85.5
Modern		8680	0.3	3.3	6.6	13.2	23.5	22.6	19.6	7.2	0.5	3.52	23.4	96.3		3.18	22.8	3.19	20.3
Maintained	All pupils	259033	2.3	10.7	12.0	16.2	19.6	16.0	13.7	6.0	0.9	4.21	41.2	96.6		3.90	39.9	3.89	38.3
	Boys	119029	1.5	7.5	9.3	14.3	19.6	18.1	17.2	8.3	1.3	3.83	32.7	95.9		3.52	32.2	3.50	30.3
	Girls	140004	3.1	13.3	14.3	17.8	19.7	14.2	10.8	4.1	0.5	4.52	48.5	97.2		4.21	46.2	4.19	44.4
All Subjects Maintained	All pupils		2.1	8.4	16.4	20.5	18.9	14.5	10.2	4.5	1.5	4.40	47.4	95.5		4.12	46.3	4.14	45.0

1 Aged 15 on 31/8/93
2 1992 results include a small amount of data from special schools
3 Calculated on basis A*=8, A=7, B=6, C=5, D=4, E=3, F=2, G=1

– less than 100 candidates
* more than 100 and less than 500 candidates
x information not available

GCSE results for 15 year olds¹ for German 1994

Type of School		Number of 15¹ year old pupils entered	Percentages achieving grades									Average points score³	% A*-C grades	% A*-G grades	1993 Average points score³	1993 % A-C grades	1992² Average points score³	1992² % A-C grades
			A*	A	B	C	D	E	F	G	U							
Comprehensive		91359	2.5	12.9	15.0	18.9	17.9	13.1	10.6	5.8	1.3	4.47	49.3	96.6	4.21	47.2	4.24	46.8
Selective		6145	10.5	36.5	25.3	16.7	7.6	2.3	0.8	0.1	0.0	6.15	89.0	99.8	6.02	88.4	5.94	87.3
Modern		1030	0.5	4.8	7.7	15.7	23.3	15.6	16.4	11.0	2.4	3.64	28.6	95.0	3.41	27.8	3.47	28.0
Maintained	All pupils	98534	2.9	14.3	15.5	18.8	17.3	12.4	10.0	5.5	1.2	4.57	51.5	96.8	4.32	49.6	4.33	48.9
	Boys	44792	1.8	10.1	12.7	17.7	18.6	14.7	12.7	7.6	1.8	4.18	42.3	95.9	3.93	41.1	3.93	40.2
	Girls	53742	3.9	17.8	17.9	19.7	16.3	10.5	7.8	3.8	0.7	4.89	59.2	97.6	4.64	56.6	4.62	55.3
All Subjects Maintained	All pupils		2.1	8.4	16.4	20.5	18.9	14.5	10.2	4.5	1.5	4.40	47.4	95.5	4.12	46.3	4.14	45.0

1 Aged 15 on 31/8/93
2 1992 results include a small amount of data from special schools
3 Calculated on basis A*=8, A=7, B=6, C=5, D=4, E=3, F=2, G=1

− less than 100 candidates
* more than 100 and less than 500 candidates
x information not available

GCSE results for 15 year olds[1] for Spanish 1994

Type of School		Number of 15[1] year old pupils entered	1994 Percentages achieving grades									Average points score[3]	% A*-C grades	% A*-G grades	1993 Average points score[3]	1993 % A-C grades	1992[2] Average points score[3]	1992[2] % A-C grades
			A*	A	B	C	D	E	F	G	U							
Comprehensive		21514	1.9	11.1	12.1	14.8	16.5	14.3	14.8	9.4	2.0	4.08	40.0	95.0	3.84	39.4	3.90	38.5
Selective		1431	10.6	39.1	26.7	15.2	5.4	1.7	0.8	0.2	0.0	6.25	91.5	99.7	5.92	86.9	6.06	89.5
Modern		681	0.7	6.8	8.1	10.9	17.8	17.8	21.4	10.6	3.8	3.55	26.4	94.0	3.35	28.6	3.73	29.6
Maintained	All pupils	23626	2.4	12.7	12.9	14.7	15.8	13.7	14.2	8.9	2.0	4.20	42.7	95.2	3.95	41.9	4.00	40.9
	Boys	9549	1.8	9.2	10.0	12.4	15.4	14.8	17.6	12.4	3.0	3.79	33.4	93.6	3.40	31.0	3.52	31.4
	Girls	14077	2.8	15.1	14.8	16.4	16.1	12.9	11.8	6.5	1.3	4.48	49.0	96.3	4.30	48.8	4.28	46.2
All Subjects Maintained	All pupils		2.1	8.4	16.4	20.5	18.9	14.5	10.2	4.5	1.5	4.40	47.4	95.5	4.12	46.3	4.14	45.0

1 Aged 15 on 31/8/93
2 1992 results include a small amount of data from special schools
3 Calculated on basis A*=8, A=7, B=6, C=5, D=4, E=3, F=2, G=1

- less than 100 candidates
* more than 100 and less than 500 candidates
x information not available

24

GCSE results for 15 year olds¹ for French, German, Spanish & other languages 1994

1994

Type of School		Number of 15¹ year old pupils entered	Percentages achieving grades									Average points score³	% A*–C grades	% A*–G grades
			A*	A	B	C	D	E	F	G	U			
Comprehensive		362384	2.1	11.0	12.6	16.9	19.1	15.2	13.1	6.3	1.1	4.09	42.6	96.4
Selective		21090	11.2	37.5	24.5	15.9	7.5	2.3	0.8	0.1	0.0	6.17	89.0	99.7
Modern		10614	0.4	4.0	7.0	13.4	22.9	21.4	19.2	7.7	0.9	3.42	24.8	96.1
Maintained	All pupils	394088	2.6	12.2	13.1	16.7	18.6	14.7	12.6	6.0	1.0	4.18	44.6	96.5
	Boys	179169	1.7	8.7	10.4	15.1	18.9	16.8	15.8	8.3	1.5	3.78	35.9	95.7
	Girls	214919	3.4	15.1	15.3	18.1	18.3	12.9	10.0	4.1	0.6	4.51	51.9	97.2
All Subjects Maintained	All pupils		2.1	8.4	16.4	20.5	18.9	14.5	10.2	4.5	1.5	4.40	47.4	95.5

1 Aged 15 on 31/8/93
2 1992 results include a small amount of data from special schools
3 Calculated on basis A*=8, A=7, B=6, C=5, D=4, E=3, F=2, G=1

– less than 100 candidates
* more than 100 and less than 500 candidates
x information not available

25

Annex B

GCE AS results for French 1994

Type of School		Number of candidates	Percentages achieving grades							% A–B grades	% A–E grades	Average points score^p	% A–B grades	% A–E grades	% A–B grades	% A–E grades
			A	B	C	D	E	N	U							
										1994			**1993**		**1992**	
Maintained	All pupils	878	9.5	8.8	12.4	17.3	19.0	14.9	16.2	18.2	67.0	1.7	14.6	64.5	18.2	64.8
	Boys	358	12.8	12.6	15.4	17.0	14.2	11.7	13.7	25.4	72.1	2.1	20.0	69.6	21.2	69.9
	Girls	520	7.1	6.2	10.4	17.5	22.3	17.1	17.9	13.3	63.5	1.5	11.8	61.9	16.5	61.7
All subjects Maintained	All pupils		7.1	10.2	14.8	17.9	18.2	12.9	15.1	17.3	68.2	1.8	17.0	65.5	16.6	65.4

– less than 100 candidates

* more than 100 and less than 500 candidates

p Calculated on basis A=5, B=4, C=3, D=2, E=1

The number of pupils taking AS levels is insufficient to yield a meaningful analysis by type of maintained school

GCE AS results for German* 1994

| Type of School | | Number of candidates | Percentages achieving grades | | | | | | | % A–B grades | % A–E grades | Average points score[p] | 1993 % A–B grades | 1993 % A–E grades | 1992 % A–B grades | 1992 % A–E grades |
			A	B	C	D	E	N	U							
Maintained	All pupils	373	12.3	11.8	14.7	15.0	18.8	14.7	11.0	24.1	72.7	2.0	19.4	70.8	18.3	75.5
	Boys	140	12.9	11.4	15.7	17.1	20.0	12.9	10.0	24.3	77.1	2.1	24.7	74.1	21.1	81.6
	Girls	233	12.0	12.0	14.2	13.7	18.0	15.9	11.6	24.0	70.0	2.0	16.3	68.8	16.3	70.7
All subjects Maintained	All pupils		7.1	10.2	14.8	17.9	18.2	12.9	15.1	17.3	68.2	1.8	17.0	65.5	16.6	65.4

– less than 100 candidates

* more than 100 and less than 500 candidates

p Calculated on basis A=5, B=4, C=3, D=2, E=1

The number of pupils taking AS levels is insufficient to yield a meaningful analysis by type of maintained school

GCE AS results for Spanish* 1994

Type of School		Number of candidates	Percentages achieving grades A	B	C	D	E	N	U	% A-B grades	% A-E grades	Average points score[p]	1993 % A-B grades	1993 % A-E grades	1992 % A-B grades	1992 % A-E grades
Maintained	All pupils	100	11.0	8.0	13.0	17.0	14.0	16.0	20.0	19.0	63.0	1.7	–	–	23.9	62.4
	Boys	29	–	–	–	–	–	–	–	–	–	–	–	–	–	–
	Girls	71	–	–	–	–	–	–	–	–	–	–	–	–	–	–
All subjects Maintained	All pupils		7.1	10.2	14.8	17.9	18.2	12.9	15.1	17.3	68.2	17.0	16.6	65.5	–	65.4

– less than 100 candidates

* more than 100 and less than 500 candidates

p Calculated on basis A=5, B=4, C=3, D=2, E=1

The number of pupils taking AS levels is insufficient to yield a meaningful analysis by type of maintained school

GCE AS results for French, German, Spanish & other languages 1994

| Type of School | | Number of candidates | Percentages achieving grades | | | | | | | % A–B grades | % A–E grades | Average points score[p] |
			A	B	C	D	E	N	U			
								1994				
Maintained	All pupils	1378	10.2	9.4	13.3	16.8	18.8	14.9	14.7	19.7	68.5	1.8
	Boys	532	12.6	11.8	15.2	17.7	15.4	12.0	13.5	24.4	72.7	2.1
	Girls	846	3.7	7.9	12.1	16.2	20.9	16.7	15.5	16.7	65.8	1.7
All subjects												
Maintained	All pupils		7.1	10.2	14.8	17.9	18.2	12.9	15.1	17.3	68.2	1.8

– less than 100 candidates

* more than 100 and less than 500 candidates

p Calculated on basis A=5, B=4, C=3, D=2, E=1

The number of pupils taking AS levels is insufficient to yield a meaningful analysis by type of maintained school

GCE A-Level results for French 1994

Type of School		Number of candidates	Percentages achieving grades							% A–B grades	% A–E grades	1993 % A–B grades	1993 % A–E grades	1992 % A–B grades	1992 % A–E grades
			A	B	C	D	E	N	U						
Comprehensive		8865	13.5	15.1	18.4	19.4	16.7	10.2	6.1	28.6	83.2	27.4	82.8	28.1	82.6
Selective		2468	21.5	19.1	20.5	18.9	12.0	4.9	2.5	40.6	92.0	38.6	92.1	38.7	91.0
Modern		71	–	–	–	–	–	–	–	–	–	–	–	18.8	69.1
Maintained	All pupils	11404	15.2	15.9	18.9	19.2	15.7	9.1	5.4	31.1	85.0	29.7	84.7	29.9	83.9
	Boys	2922	16.3	15.3	18.5	18.6	16.2	9.3	5.1	31.6	84.9	30.5	85.7	31.5	83.9
	Girls	8482	14.9	16.1	19.0	19.4	15.6	9.1	5.4	31.0	85.0	29.4	84.4	29.4	83.9
All subjects Maintained	All pupils		13.1	16.2	18.5	18.9	15.2	9.4	7.5	29.3	81.9	28.0	79.7	26.4	78.6

– less than 100 candidates

* more than 100 and less than 500 candidates

GCE A-Level results for German 1994

Type of School	Number of candidates	1994 Percentages achieving grades							% A–B grades	% A–E grades	1993 % A–B grades	1993 % A–E grades	1992 % A–B grades	1992 % A–E grades
		A	B	C	D	E	N	U						
Comprehensive	3873	15.1	16.6	18.2	19.0	16.4	8.9	5.4	31.7	85.3	32.1	83.0	30.4	82.3
Selective	902	22.3	24.2	19.0	17.5	12.2	3.4	1.1	46.5	95.1	43.9	92.4	41.7	93.1
Modern	22	–	–	–	–	–	–	–	–	–	–	–	–	–
Maintained All pupils	4797	16.4	18.1	18.4	18.7	15.6	7.9	4.5	34.5	87.2	34.5	84.9	32.0	83.9
Boys	1324	17.0	18.2	18.6	17.4	16.1	9.0	3.3	35.2	87.3	35.2	84.4	35.2	84.5
Girls	3473	16.2	13.0	18.3	19.2	15.4	7.5	5.0	34.2	87.1	34.2	85.0	31.0	83.7
All subjects Maintained All pupils		13.1	16.2	18.5	18.9	15.2	9.4	7.5	29.3	81.9	28.0	79.7	26.4	78.6

– less than 100 candidates

* more than 100 and less than 500 candidates

GCE A-Level results for Spanish 1994

Type of School		Number of candidates	Percentages achieving grades							1994		1993		1992	
			A	B	C	D	E	N	U	% A–B grades	% A–E grades	% A–B grades	% A–E grades	% A–B grades	% A–E grades
Comprehensive		993	18.8	21.3	20.0	14.8	10.4	7.5	5.7	40.2	85.4	33.6	84.7	35.6	87.8
Selective		263	17.9	25.5	25.9	17.1	9.1	1.5	2.3	43.3	95.4	43.6	91.6	41.0	88.6
Modern		15	–	–	–	–	–	–	–	–	–	–	–	–	–
Maintained	All pupils	1271	18.5	22.1	21.1	15.7	10.2	6.2	5.0	40.6	87.6	35.7	86.3	36.7	88.1
	Boys	314	24.8	25.2	17.2	11.8	8.0	5.4	4.8	50.0	86.9	36.2	85.9	37.8	89.5
	Girls	957	16.4	21.1	22.4	16.9	11.0	6.5	5.0	37.5	87.8	35.6	86.4	36.3	87.6
All subjects Maintained	All pupils		13.1	16.2	18.5	18.9	15.2	9.4	7.5	29.3	81.9	28.0	79.7	26.4	78.6

– less than 100 candidates

* more than 100 and less than 500 candidates

GCE A-Level results for French, German, Spanish & other languages 1994

Type of School		Number of candidates	1994							% A–B grades	% A–E grades
			Percentages achieving grades								
			A	B	C	D	E	N	U		
Comprehensive		14438	14.6	16.2	18.6	18.8	15.9	9.4	5.8	30.8	84.1
Selective		3719	21.6	20.8	20.6	18.3	11.7	4.2	2.1	42.5	93.1
Modern		119	7.6	16.0	22.7	15.1	17.6	13.4	7.6	23.5	79.0
Maintained	All pupils	18276	16.0	17.1	19.0	18.7	15.1	8.4	5.1	33.1	85.9
	Boys	4846	17.3	16.9	18.6	17.7	15.3	8.6	4.8	34.2	85.8
	Girls	13430	15.5	17.2	19.1	19.0	15.0	8.3	5.2	32.7	85.9
All subjects Maintained	All pupils		13.1	16.2	18.5	18.9	15.2	9.4	7.5	29.3	81.9

– less than 100 candidates

* more than 100 and less than 500 candidates

Printed in the United Kingdom for HMSO
Dd300287 4/95 C130 G3397 10170